One misty day Jelly saw a rabbit on the grass.
It looked like Jet, the pet, but it ran away.

Jelly ran after it.

She saw it go into a clump of long grass at one end of the log. It did not come out.

Jelly went to the clump of long grass. She looked in it.

She saw a tunnel.

The tunnel went into the log.

Jelly crept into the tunnel.

She felt something soft and fluffy.

She jumped up. Was it Jet, the pet?

Then lots of soft fluffy things rushed past her. Oh no!
Jelly went back along the tunnel.

She pushed past the clump of long grass. She was in the mist.
She looked up. She saw seven little rabbits on the grass.

The rabbit like Jet was next to them. She looked very cross. "You clumsy cat," she said. "You trod on one of my little rabbits."

"Do not go into my tunnel again," she said. "It is my nest for my little rabbits. Go away."

Jelly ran away into the mist. She was very sorry.